CW00613341

WHAT SELENA SAYS

THE UNOFFICIAL COLLECTION

WHAT

SELENA

SAYS

Quadrille

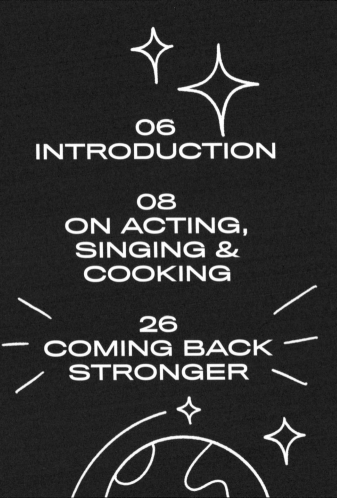

Starting out as an actress on the Disney Channel, Selena Gomez evolved into a singer, carving out her own brand of quirky pop with hits like 'Same Old Love' and 'Bad Liar'. From there, she has become a TV cook with her show *Selena + Chef*, spent time as the world's most-followed woman on Instagram, and had some high-profile relationships along the way. But she's also struggled with physical and mental health issues that put her in hospital. Since releasing a documentary about her experience with bipolar disorder, Selena has found a new superpower: vulnerability. She has become an icon of kindness and inner strength, inspiring people to talk about their own struggles. Now at the peak of her career, with hit songs and huge TV shows like *Only Murders in the Building*, Selena cares most about happiness, surrounding herself with love, and living life to the fullest.

On Acting,

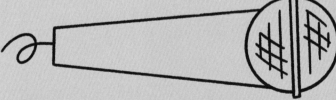

Singing

"I started working when
I was seven. I quickly
learned how to play
the part. I have juggled
work and school and
relationships for as long as
I can remember. As great
as life was, underneath
all of it I was struggling."

"There's this misconception of the 'child star' – that they don't make their own decisions, that they don't have their own identity. Now more than ever, I <u>want to claim</u> every <u>choice I've made</u>."

"I still live with this haunting feeling that people still view me as this Disney girl."

"That was my job, in a way. To be perfect."

"Once Disney was over,
I was like,
'Oh, sh*t.' I didn't know
what I wanted to be.
I had to learn to
be myself."

"My mom always told me,
'If this isn't fun for you,
we're done.
You can quit at any time.'
It never felt like
I had to do it.
♥ I loved acting." ♥

"I never really intended on being a singer full time, but apparently that hobby turned into something else."

"I don't think I'm the best singer, but I do know how to tell stories and I love being able to make songs."

"One of the greatest parts of being able to sing and to write music is that I get to be vulnerable. The only thing I can write about, usually, is power and love."

"I love every choice
that I've made. Because
now I understand how to
apply that to my music.
This is who I am. I'm glad
my life was never perfect."

"Nothing makes me happier than 90 minutes of being with my fans and just celebrating together."

"I love being in the studio. Because the first hour [...] I just talk. It's like therapy."

"People who know me, know that I love to cook, except I have no idea what to do or how to do it."

"I was like: 'What is
something I can put out
in the world that can
make people laugh,
or make people smile?'
And what do I love more
than anything? Food."

"I had to really discover what was going to work for me because there were times in my career where I sang things that just <u>weren't me</u> and weren't for me. You can hear it in my voice."

"I would maybe love to write something; I'd maybe love to direct something."

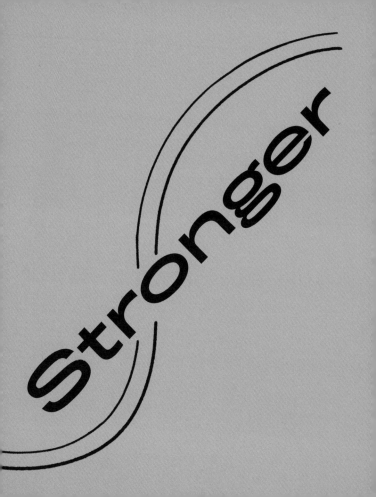

"I have lupus and deal with kidney issues and high blood pressure, so I deal with <u>a lot</u> of health issues."

"After years of
going through a lot
of different things,
I realized that
I was bipolar.
When I have
more information,
it actually helps me,
it doesn't <u>scare me</u>
<u>once I know it."</u>

"I had to stop because I had <u>everything</u> and I was absolutely <u>broken inside</u>. I kept it all together enough to where I would never let you down, but I kept it too much together <u>to where I let myself down</u>."

"The psychotic break,
as much as it was painful,
actually led me to
discovering my diagnosis.
I sought help.
I believe in medication.
It has completely
changed my life."

"If you are broken, you do not have to stay broken."

"I don't have anything to hide."

"I would much rather talk about what's going on in our real lives than pretend to be happy."

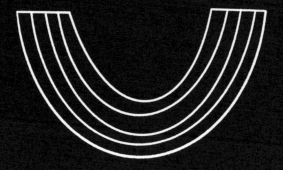

"It would be so
unrealistic for me to
be in pain and then
release a song where
I'm like, 'Life is awesome
and this is great!'"

"I love who I am,
and I love how my
mind works,
because it is who I am.
But I am so grateful
that I now have a better
relationship with it."

"It's OK
to feel
not good
enough
and to feel
like you're
complicated
and
complex."

"I also struggle with my own thoughts and feelings at times. But this <u>does not</u> make me faulty, this <u>does not</u> make me weak. This does <u>not</u> make me less than. This makes me human."

"The world needs to know that mental health matters. It's just as important as your physical health."

"I actually truly feel like the older I've gotten, the more I've really <u>appreciated</u> the <u>struggles</u> that I've had."

"I am happier, I am healthier, and I am in control of my emotions and thoughts more than I have ever been."

"If you can't accept me at my happiest, then don't be in my life at all."

"I know what's best for me and I will fight till I get what I deserve."

On

Relationships

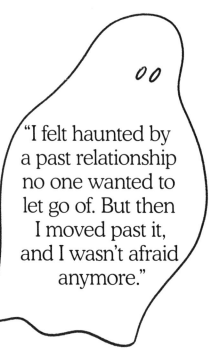

"I felt haunted by a past relationship no one wanted to let go of. But then I moved past it, and I wasn't afraid anymore."

"A lot of people are afraid
of being alone and I
probably tortured myself
in my head for, like,
two years being alone,
and then I kind
of accepted it.
Then I came up
with my plan,
which was I was
going to adopt at 35,
if I had not met anyone."

"[My boyfriend] isn't my only source of happiness. I was alone for five years, and I got really used to it."

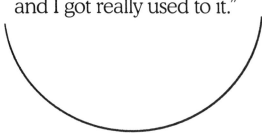

"[Love] just happens when you least expect it."

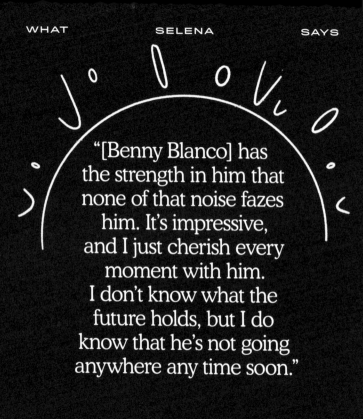

"[Benny Blanco] has the strength in him that none of that noise fazes him. It's impressive, and I just cherish every moment with him. I don't know what the future holds, but I do know that he's not going anywhere any time soon."

"I love having level-headed people around that couldn't give two f*cks about what I do."

"We are here for relationships,
for people just like us
who feel worthless.
Your purpose is to
share, help, encourage.
Remember that."

"Taylor [Swift] makes
me feel empowered,
like I can trust new people [...]
The way she cares about
women is so adamant.
It's pulling me out
of my shell."

"In this season of my life, I want to be loved the way I love people, I want to give the way people give so generously to me and I want to continue to work on becoming a better and a happier person every day."

"It's all about, at the end of the day, for me, owning my power and I am who I surround myself with."

"I've basically grown up in front of everyone."

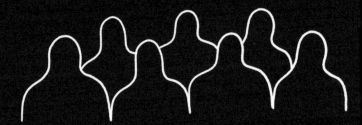

"I love working and it distracts me from bad things."

"I love my job, I do what I do, so I just want to give my all to [the fans]."

"I feel <u>safe</u> with my fans. I'm going to meet every single one of them. They're the goodness of what I do."

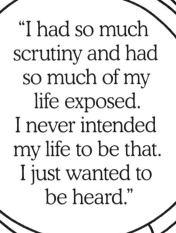

"I had so much scrutiny and had so much of my life exposed. I never intended my life to be that. I just wanted to be heard."

"There's been so much,
especially with women
in this industry,
just being pitted
against other women
[...] we are our
own people."

"I can't care anymore that people are going to twist my words or talk about it. Everybody said every <u>single thing</u> they could say about me."

"I just don't care about the noise anymore. It drives me crazy."

"Ultimately, people – I'm referring to the media, and then I'll be done talking about them because it frustrates me – just want me to be this evil person that I'm not. It's the whole 'build you up and knock you down' thing."

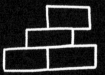

"I had to do a lot of
work on myself to say,
'If I lost all this tomorrow,
I'd be fine. I could
open up a coffee
shop and do a play
every other month.'"

"I need my life to not be dictated by these people that I don't even know."

"When I'm onstage
or in front of a crowd,
I'll always find the one
person who <u>doesn't</u>
like me. And I'll
believe *them.* I want
to believe in myself."

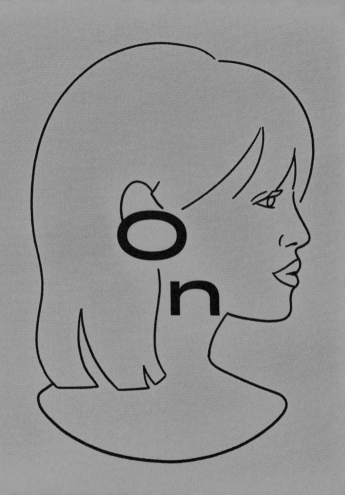

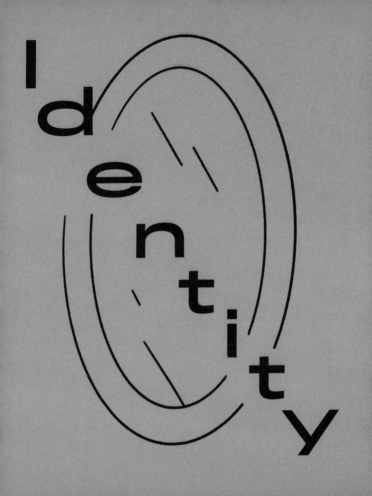

"I don't have life figured out by all means, but I have a great family."

"In the 1970s, my aunt crossed the border from Mexico to the United States hidden in the back of a truck. My grandparents followed, and my father was born in Texas soon after. In 1992, I was born a U.S. citizen, thanks to their bravery and sacrifice."

"Undocumented immigration is an issue I think about every day, and I never forget how blessed I am to have been born in this country, thanks to my family and the grace of circumstance."

"As a Mexican-American woman, I feel a responsibility to use my platform to be a voice for people who are too afraid to speak."

"I don't know how to
be anything but myself.
The most important thing
is that we learn and we
continue to learn from
each other. Please stay
true to yourself. Please
just remain who you are."

"The only thing that worries
me is how much value people
our age place on social media.
It's an incredible platform,
but in a lot of ways it's given
young people, myself included,
a false representation
of what's important."

"It does more than knock
the wind out of you,
it crushes you, when
people try to tell you
you're not good enough.
And it almost did for me,
but there was my mom
next to me, stronger than
ever. And she said the
most important thing is
to always trust in myself."

"You should never stop figuring out who you are."

The

of

"No cares about what you're doing. It's about who I am, and being okay with where I am. I am grateful to be alive."

"I turned
the bad
things into
a good
thing."

"If I'm doing something because I love it, I should do it, because I love it and I believe I can do it."

"Please, please be kinder to everyone and consider others' mental health."

"I work hard, and anyone that you ever talk to that's worked with me knows I'm _professional_, _kind_ and that I care about people."

"My mom has always taught me, every single time, turn my cheek the other way. It is always the best feeling waking up the next day going, 'They gave me their worst, I gave them my best, and that's all I can do.'"

"Once I stopped, and accepted my vulnerability, and decided to share my story with people – that's when I felt release."

"I'm focusing on what really matters."

"I don't need to do anything other than love myself, take care of my work, fans, family and friends."

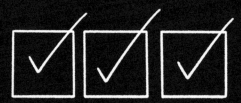

"Kindness always wins."

"I'm choosing myself over anything else."

"I haven't even touched the surface of what I want to do."

SOURCES

Billboard,
8th October 2015
– pp. **15, 53, 61**

Elle,
29th September 2015
– p. **11**

Giving Back Generation,
TaTaTu, 31st May 2022
– p. **28**

Harper's Bazaar, 7th February
2018 – p. **92**

Instagram [@selenagomez] –
pp. **39, 43, 52, 89,
90, 91**

Instagram Live with Miley
Cyrus [@mileycyrus],
4th April 2020
– p. **29**

On Purpose with Jay Shetty,
iHeartPodcasts
– p. **54**

Onstage at the American Music
Awards, 20th November 2016
– pp. **30, 32**

Onstage at the Rare Beauty
Mental Health Summit,
1st May 2024 – p. **55**

Onstage at WE Day California,
2013 – pp. **76, 78, 84**

People,
4th October 2023
– p. **40**

Rolling Stone,
4th January 2016
– p.**19**

Selena + Chef,
HBO Max, 2022
– pp. **18, 22**

Selena Gomez: My Mind & Me,
Apple TV +, 2022
– pp. **10, 31, 33, 34, 36,
37, 38, 41, 46, 69, 79,
82**

SmartLess, Apple Podcasts,
8th January 2024
– pp. **16, 17, 59**

Quadrille, Penguin Random House UK, One Embassy Gardens, 8 Viaduct Gardens, London SW11 7BW

Quadrille Publishing Limited is part of the Penguin Random House group of companies whose addresses can be found at global. penguinrandomhouse.com

Published by Quadrille in 2025

www.penguin.co.uk

A CIP catalogue record for this book is available from the British Library

ISBN 9781784887476

10 9 8 7 6 5 4 3 2 1

Publishing Director: Kajal Mistry
Senior Commissioning Editor: Kate Burkett
Editorial Assistant: Harriet Thornley
Design and Illustration: Double Slice Studio (Amelia Leuzzi and Bonnie Eichelberger)
Senior Production Controller: Martina Georgieva

Colour reproduction by p2d

Printed in China by RR Donnelley Asia Printing Solution Limited

The authorised representative in the EEA is Penguin Random House Ireland, Morrison Chambers, 32 Nassau Street, Dublin D02 YH68.